CW01560477

POEMS, ODES, LYRICS

POEMS, ODES, LYRICS

by
Merlin Parrington

To Katya
Happy Reading
Merlin

ARTHUR H. STOCKWELL LTD
Torrs Park   Ilfracombe   Devon
Established 1898
www.ahstockwell.co.uk

© Merlin Parrington, 2010
First published in Great Britain, 2010
All rights reserved.
No part of this publication may be reproduced
or transmitted in any form or by any means,
electronic or mechanical, including photocopy,
recording, or any information storage and
retrieval system, without permission
in writing from the copyright holder.

British Library Cataloguing-in-Publication Data.
A catalogue record for this book is available
from the British Library.

ISBN 978-0-7223-4003-5
Printed in Great Britain by
Arthur H. Stockwell Ltd
Torrs Park   Ilfracombe
Devon

CONTENTS

A COUNTRY WALK

Among the hills where I long to roam,
Where the grass is green and overgrown,
With a gentle breeze blowing through my hair
I wander onward without a care.

The wooded copses enriched with time
Stand elegantly mature like a glass of red wine,
And the birds of the air object to my intrusion
As they rise from the ground in utter profusion.

The wild flowers grow untouched and untamed;
Some are known whilst others are unnamed.
The hedgerows are full of berries and seeds
Where the birds of the air settle and feed.

On and on through this meadowland
I walk contented hand in hand,
With nature's fingers entwined in mine.
I'm intoxicated in the warm sunshine.

The rolling hills stretch on and on
As the chirping of insects falls into song.
It is nature's way of telling me
The hillsides are there for all to see.

THOUGHTS

Think not yet upon how life could be
Nor cast your thoughts on life that's gone,
But dream on life with the sweetest thoughts
And you will have something to look upon.

Think, but don't make thoughts your master
Nor dream upon things that should have been,
But look upon life with a purposeful hope
On things to come and yet unseen.

Waste not your time on unforgiving thoughts
Nor how two wrongs don't make a right,
But dwell upon how sweet life can be
When only your thoughts come to light.

When life's dark pathways turn to light
And your problems become the lighter,
Think back upon the good thoughts you had
And the world will seem all the brighter.

Don't indulge your thoughts in dreaming dreams
Nor dwell upon thoughts too long,
But make a point in thinking things out
And you will have something to look upon.

THE DESERT RAT
(British 8th Army)

We made our way yard by yard across the sandy sea
To where we had been once before, I remember.
With sand-sweat brows and caked-up clothes
We dragged ourselves along, I remember,
To where our dugout used to be,
Waiting another onslaught of artillery, I remember.

On the word of command we moved yet again
Slowly across a minefield, I remember,
Where Eddie, my chum, died where he lay
As a mine ripped open his guts, I remember.
I looked to where his body had been
To know I'd never be the same, I remember.

The advance was torture, if not hell,
As I made my dugout alone, I remember;
And I cried, as my youngster cries,
With relief of another day, I remember.
Then I prayed to God I was spared
Of Eddie's tragedy to tell – I remember.

THE NATIONAL SERVICEMAN

I've served my term in the army,
At home in barracks and abroad.
I've finished my national-service term –
Two years of it, thank God!
I've been to many lands whilst serving
In the army of the King;
I've been to lands unthought of,
Now home to England I bring
My two long years of adventure,
My tales of far away,
Of the thoughts I shall always carry
And the mates and friends I made.
In the last few months of my service
In the army of the Queen
To serve my term under two sovereigns
Was something I hadn't foreseen.
But it's just one of the tales of my service
To tell now that my term is done –
Thoughts which I shall always carry
And the friendships I have won.

THE RED BERETS
(Men of Arnhem)

They fall not like others fall,
The Red Devils from the sky.
They fought just like others fought –
These soldiers from on high.

Red beret was their headgear,
Wings graced their tunics brown,
Their badge a symbol of fame –
These soldiers of the Crown.

Gliders took them in their scores,
And parachutes brought them down
On the battles' fields where they fought –
These soldiers of the Crown.

These men fought to keep the peace –
Saviours of Arnhem town.
Raise your glass for ever in salute –
These soldiers of the Crown.

Men trained but God protected
These Red Devils from the sky.
They fought just like others fought;
They died as others died.

49TH FOOT

We've seen service in many a land
Too numerous to mention right now;
We've seen battalions come and go,
But we are always last somehow.

We're tough, rugged and under strength,
But yet we're smart when we should.
We've roamed the mountains of Africa,
We lads of Berkshire who could.

Shifta who lived in the mountains –
Cattle thieves and murderers they were,
Terrorising the natives and villages,
But we lads of Berkshire could cure.

Some of the lads got killed by these,
Some on 'un decorated too.
These lads they died for their country,
But Berkshire will remember those few.

Now Shiftas have gone to a land beyond;
We lads of Berkshire 'ave done.
We've gone to a place with no disgrace,
Our tour of duty well done.

ONE IN A MILLION

I'm just a soldier.
Like many a chap,
I've travelled the world
And want to come back
To the life I led before the war,
To mother, wife and friends I adore.
I've had my fun
And I've had my jokes.
I've lost my mates and other blokes –
Chaps I slept with and had my meals,
To see them fight
And fall at my heels.
But now it's over,
And time has flown by,
I'm home again with mother,
Wife and friends close by.

SPEARHEAD

The 1st Division of the British Army
Stationed in MELF
Came from lands far and near
Into Egypt's land of unrest.
We came in brigades fighting fit –
The 1st, 2nd and 3rd –
Fighting men of the motherland.
Of us you have surely heard (Spearhead).
We are all of one the three of us
On our way to Gyppo's shore,
Coming to settle an argument
Once and for evermore.
Egypt and Persia have joined hands,
Hoping to conquer the land,
Claiming the rights of the Suez Canal
And Farouk, King of the Sudan.
They have given us a task to do –
More work for the boys to endure –
To keep the word of England true
And the name of our army pure.
They have taken us from our families,
From our home, love and kin,
To fight for our rights in Egypt
Under the command of General Erskine.

AN UNFINISHED PRAYER

Angel above, look down on me,
Brighten my days so I might see.
Come – lead me by thy hand,
Deliver me into thy land.
Enough have I sinned and done Thee wrong:
Father in heaven hear this my psalm.
Give me Your grace so I might learn,
Help me to find the love I yearn.
In time to come, I know I shall be;
Judge me then when I am free.
Keep me in Your faith so true,
Let me live on high with You.
Mighty heavens, how bright you look!
Need have I as I Your holy book.
Open Your gates for I am here;
Paternal One, are You near?
Quotidian, I prayed for this day;
Reach out so Your hand doth lay
Softly on mine and bid me home.
Tender Lord, no more I roam;
Unite me with the ones I seek.
Virgin Mother, to thee I weep –
Watch over me in my home on high.
Heavenly Father, for Thee I die.

THE VALLEY OF DEATH

This little hamlet of much renown
My Lynmouth town,
Was heaven's rest to all within
Free from fear and sin.
But in the valley the rain came
Beneath a shadow of a cloud,
Bringing destruction to those within
Unknown it came – not loud.
Taking with it its loss of life.
Its churches, homes and all in sight
Still the flourishing rains did come,
Upon this frightened village at night.
Down the mountain the monster came
Swirling homesteads and floating trees,
The crazy village within its mouth,
Their cries of pain – their death plea.
And yet their courage to behold
Oh God Our Help in Ages Past – their song
Yet in their hearts there was no wrong.
Through the cloud the sun shone down
My Lynmouth town
Torture have we suffered here,
Through death and fear,
But all England is by our side.
Oh God with us abide!

SPRINGTIME

Springtime and love-time –
A season of greetings,
Birds wildly chirping
And children at play,
Sunshine and flowers to welcome each day.

May time and playtime –
A reason for meeting,
Lovers are mating
At each other's love call,
Children are dancing around the maypole.

Daytime and night-time –
A love is recaptured.
New love found new love
When I found you.
Sweethearts and lovers are starting anew.

Your time and my time –
A time for singing.
Wedding bells are ringing
This happy morn.
Springtime has come and love is reborn.

REBECCA'S LABRADOR

As a little puppy I was taken away
To a house with others like me.
I was trained to help in many ways
Blind people who couldn't see.
I was taught the way of how to guide,
On buses, streets and in the town,
Carefully avoiding the traffic,
And when in danger lie down.

My mistress I will always obey;
She depends on me for her sight.
I listen to everything she tells me,
For in her darkness I am her light.
In return for all I can give,
Her love for me is deep.
She gives me a home in which to live
And a bed on which I can sleep.

OH, MOUNTAIN!
(Grossglockner, Austria)

Mighty in majesty,
Powerful in height,
Silent in daytime
And covered in white,
To look upon gracefully,
Mighty mountain so high!
Through clouds you are looking
High up to the sky
With perfect serenity.
Oh, mountain supreme,
With a white-covered coat
For ever have been.
The years have gone by;
You've always stood fast.
So we bow to your presence
This day until last.

MY SCOTTISH LASSIE

Like a snowdrop lily-white,
Like the stars which shine at night,
Like the purple heather on the hill,
My Scottish lassie smileth still.

Like a gem that sparkles bright,
Like a bird upon its flight,
Like the Scottish hills around,
A bonny lassie's heart I've found.

Like the sky of royal blue,
Like the early morning dew,
Like a snowdrop when it falls,
My bonny lassie calls.

Like all heaven is upon us,
Like all earthly things are done,
Like a new love which has borne me,
A bonny lassie's heart I've won.

With a true love I will love her,
With faithfulness I will live,
With only my heart to offer,
But my heart I dearly give.

WHAT A WONDERFUL DAY!
(A Christmas carol)

Peace, peace, perfect peace
Was the start of the first Christmas Day.
A child of God was given to man;
On straw in a manger He lay.

Chorus:
What a wonderful day when Jesus was born!
What a wonderful, wonderful day!
He came to us as the Holy Ghost –
Christ Jesus came to stay.

Joy, joy, wonderful joy!
He gave to all who came in,
To find he was the Holy Ghost,
Sent to forgive us our sin.

Chorus.

Love, love, infinite love
This Christmas time shall I give
To Jesus Christ, My only Son,
Sent so others might live.

Chorus.

Christ Jesus came to stay.
Christ Jesus came to stay.
Christ Jesus came to stay.

THE BATTLE IS OVER

When the battle is over
And the fight is won,
I home with my Lord
And my life's begun.

Chorus:
When I walk with God
And I talk with Him,
My prayers are answered
And my psalm I'll sing.

My footsteps lead to heaven
Up the golden stairs.
I'll walk on and on
Because I know I'm there.

Chorus.

I will be born again
In the arms of my Lord,
And I'll live with Him
In one accord.

Chorus.

My soul is now cleansed
And my sins washed clean.
He has taken me in!
My dear Lord I've seen!

Chorus.

MARRIAGE VOWS

On the day your vows are taken
And you pledge yourselves to each other,
The awesomeness of such an occasion
Is to yourselves and no other.

Seek not to show demonstratively
That you are the better one,
But show your love in such a way
To the partner you have won.

As time passes by,
And your love grows the stronger,
Remember your vows
And love will last the longer.

Remember to kiss each morning
And be thankful for another day.
Keep showing your love to each other
Because life is happier that way.

I'M IN LOVE

I do believe that God above
Created you for me to love.
He picked you out from all the rest
Because He knew I loved you best.

I had a heart so warm and true,
But now it's gone from me to you.
Take care of it as I have done,
For now you've two and I have none.

If I go to heaven and you're not there,
I'll paint your face on the golden stair,
So all the angels can look and see
What you, my darling, meant to me.

Should you not arrive by Judgement Day,
I'll know you've gone the other way.
And just to prove what I would do,
I'd even go to hell for you.

THE PATTERN-MAKER

For all that is good
Which is made from wood –
Intricacies and the like –
For all that is best
And put to the test
Is the skill of the pattern-maker's knife.

With deftness and skill
He will carve at will
Grotesque and grandeur,
Shapes and sizes
Of all devices
From seasoned timber and mature.

The craft of old
Can now be told
For there is no other akin.
The craft that was taught
Of now there is naught,
Is now made from plastic and resin.

But, to be sure,
There are a few more
Whose skill is carved into life,
But what can be said
Of the craft that is dead
Is the skill of the pattern-maker's knife.

THE FLYING FOX

It wasn't until now did I know you were gone.
I cared not for your presence but how I was wrong,
Looking back with memories of deed you had done
Sinking the last U-boat a fame you had won.
In the First World War when the pride of the sea,
But no longer in sight just a memory to me.

The people of Bristol are proud of your name
And now that you have gone will not feel the same,
For fifty-odd years you trained men for sea
And graced our docks with supreme majesty.
The bosun'd whistle no longer sounds loud
From the decks of the ship that was once very proud.

Farewell then great ship on your voyage to sea
Your monument that was is no longer to be,
As I pass by the space you once filled with pride
There is nothing to see and nothing to hide.
Farewell then great ship your name lingers on
In the memory of those to whom you belonged.

ELIZABETH THE SECOND

Many long years we served under kings –
Great kings have reigned in our time.
They served us well, as we have them.
Now England has a queen in her prime.
England's young queen served us well –
A princess so fair in her teen
Has risen to be our sovereign lady,
Elizabeth the Second – England's queen.

With royal greetings she received us,
Her subjects loyal and true,
To serve her in her time of reign.
Elizabeth, our best respects to you!
To all who live within her realm
In England's great empire,
To serve them both in years to come –
Elizabeth and her sire.

From the golden throng she's crowned,
And her royal standard is cast.
She is proclaimed Elizabeth the Second –
England's queen until last.
God bless her, for her task is great.
Guide her with Your hand unseen,
Give her courage, health and strength.
God save our queen.

THE PASSING OF TIME

A hundred years
She graced our land,
Her humbleness supreme.
In her gracious way she served us –
Our dowager Mother Queen.

A hundred years
Of perpetual devotion
In her gentleness and charm –
A great centenarian lady
With peacefulness so calm.

A hundred years
She trod life's path
With dignity and love
She showed us all the way to live
With the help of God above.

A hundred years
She guided her life –
A creditable achievement it had been.
For fifty years and a little more
She had been our dowager Mother Queen.

OUR LAST KING GEORGE

How peaceful and still the night had been
O'er this darkened land devoured!
Our beloved king's life went unseen
As the Heavenly King placed His hand on ours.

To us our king's much honour
To his people love and grace.
To us he served with power and pride –
To us his people and race.

In his dominions overseas,
To where the English flag is cast,
We bow our heads in stillness
As the Union Jack is half-mast.

God gave him his work to do;
Great works he had endured.
We accepted his toil as our right,
But this to us he had ensured.

He passed away as day was born –
So young our king to die! –
King George the Sixth, our English lord
Who reigned evermore on high.

THE LOVE I CAPTURED

All night I lie and think of thee.
Now and then I see thee there,
In the garden where the roses bloom,
For Pauline, who cometh soon.

And as the roses fall and die
What chance have they to catch her eye?
Alas! she will not turn aside,
But into my loving arms abide.

My love for thee is at its best.
Thou hast taken my name in thankfulness,
And for thee alone I do live.
Thy loving heart thou hast give.

We will not regret the years ahead,
Our life's long path still unshed.
And in our years of heavenly bliss,
For thee, Pauline, I dearly kiss.

To live our lives side by side,
With thee, Pauline, my immortal bride,
So let's not linger whilst life is young,
But walk life's way as one.

THE LONELY GUARD

As I lay with my rifle before me
Camouflaged by the night sky,
I watched for signs of movement
As I kept a watchful eye.
I lay out there in the desert
My chin cupped in my hand,
I was keeping watch over the enemy
As my sweat dropped in the sand.
I fingered my rifle nervously
Out there in the dark of night,
When memories of home came crowded
As I was too young to fight.
My comrades lay quietly sleeping
It was my turn to keep the guard,
I was their only protector
And to keep awake was hard.